Images of Appalachian Coalfields

In the Visual Studies Series

edited by Douglas Harper

Builder Levy | Images of

Appalachian Coalfields

Introduction by Helen Matthews Lewis

Foreword by Cornell Capa

Temple University Press

Philadelphia

Temple University Press, Philadelphia 19122
Copyright © 1989 by Temple University. All rights reserved
Published 1989
Printed in Hong Kong

The paper used in this publication meets the minimum
requirements of American National Standard for Information
Sciences—Permanence of Paper for Printed Library Materials,
ANSI Z39.48-1984

Library of Congress Cataloging-in-Publication Data
Levy, Builder.
    Images of Appalachian coalfields/Builder Levy: introduction by
Helen Matthews Lewis; foreword by Cornell Capa.
    p. cm.—(Visual studies)
    ISBN 0-87722-588-5 (alk. paper)
    1. Coal miners—Appalachian Region—Pictorial works.   2. Coal
mines and mining—Appalachian Region.   I. Title.   II. Series.
HD8039.M62U6437 1989
338.7′622334′097—dc19   88-24816
                                                         CIP

My daddy was a miner
And I'm a miner's son
And I'll stick with the union
Till ev'ry battle's won.
—Florence Reece
  "Which Side Are You On?"

Contents

Foreword

I find nothing more mysterious than the behavior of documentary photographers. They doggedly pursue difficult and often surprising subjects. They willingly expend vast amounts of time and money with little hope of reimbursement. They remain undaunted in the face of hardship.

Builder Levy provides a perfect example. A New York City teacher, Levy is hardly a heroic figure. He is the last person I would expect to have undertaken a project as arduous and threatening as a study of the life and work of the Appalachian coal miner. What motivates him? Certainly not the promise of financial recompense—he may only make enough money from print and book sales to pay for gasoline on one of his many journeys through Appalachia. Yet for fourteen years Levy documented these Americans, producing images that are being seen for the first time by the readers of this book.

Levy's faithful commitment to his subjects and his passionate pursuit of memorable images from deep in the Appalachian mines is matched by the commitment of the miners he photographed. They too are committed—or condemned—to living and working in these cold, draining, primitive circumstances for compensation so minimal that one wonders what traditions compel them to persist.

Builder Levy's photographs offer us a clue. His honest documentation of life in Appalachia bears none of the exploitative marks of an outsider. His truthful and sympathetic portrait of these strong people demands our trust and demonstrates the miners' one-to-one acceptance, on human terms, of the photographer.

Levy's images are impressive. Many will doubtless hang on museum and gallery walls for years to come. Also impressive is his sense of partnership and his gratitude. Levy offers thanks to the widest variety of people, all of whom contributed to the fulfillment of his dream as a photographer. Most important, however, is what he has given back to us through his photographs.

Just look at the photographs: the old folks, Grace and George Johnson, surrounded by their neighbors' children; the Oglesbys' kitchen; men and women miners playing pool at the Montego Lounge; the determined face of a young boy at an abandoned tipple; men attending a Black Lung Association rally; the simple folk art adorning the wall of the Red Robin Inn; the hard life engraved on people's faces in a UMWA picket line; and the photograph that tells the story best—a stone marker with its stern message, "Prepare to Meet God." You have the idea. You now know what this book is about, and what the lives of these miners are like!

Many thanks, Builder Levy, for presenting us with these impressive images and thereby giving us some insight into a group of people we might not otherwise get to know.

Cornell Capa

Preface

The pictures here represent fourteen years of visiting and photo-
graphing Appalachian coal miners, their families, and their neighbors. This book allows me to share my personal vision of these
people and their environment, hidden from most of the nation in
small towns and villages tucked away in the hollows of the steep
mountains and rolling hills of West Virginia, Kentucky, and western
Pennsylvania. During summer vacations and other breaks from my
teaching job, I drove my 1966 red Volkswagen convertible throughout the coalfields, visiting the coal camps where the great struggles of
the miners had taken place: Mingo, Logan, and Raleigh counties; Paint
and Cabin Creek, Matewan, Williamson, and Scotts Run, West Virginia; Pike and Harlan counties, Kentucky; Cokeburg, Marianna, and
Ellsworth, Pennsylvania. I visited Blair Mountain where in 1921 ten
thousand armed miners, Black and white, for almost a week fought
an armed battle with coal-operator gun thugs and sheriff's deputies.
The miners were fighting for the right of their union brothers in
Logan County, West Virginia, to organize without being terrorized.
For three consecutive summers I lived in Mingo County where, in
the 1920s, the union set up tent colonies to house, clothe, and feed

the more than fifty thousand striking miners and their families who had been evicted from company houses by the coal operators. I also went to eastern Kentucky where Harry Sims, a nineteen-year-old Jewish boy from New York City, had come in 1932 to help miners unionize, and was gunned down by hired thugs of the coal-operators.

More than the mines, tipples, coal camps and company houses, old cemeteries, and churches, what made the coalfield heritage live for me were the faces of the people, the stories they shared, and their indomitable spirit. It was the trust and cooperation of the many people who opened their hearts and homes that made these photographs possible.

Coal companies, however, do not generally welcome strangers on their property; gaining access to photograph the mines was frustrating at first. Then early one July morning in 1970, in Williamson, West Virginia, I got a break. With their permission, I followed two miners driving to work in a pickup truck. I parked near the entrance in case a quick getaway was required. Then I tailed the two men as they walked toward their fellow miners waiting for the shift to begin. I approached, taking pictures, trying to make it obvious I was there to photograph. To my surprise, nobody stopped me. Miners and foremen alike were friendly and joked with me. I told them I was a teacher from New York City trying to photograph the real life of the coal miner. I returned to the mine several times during that summer, arriving before the morning and afternoon shifts.

At other mines, my reception was different. One superintendent suggested: "Why don't you go back to New York, where you came from!" Another passed down the word that "[the superintendent] doesn't want you aggravating the men anymore." And, after shooting on the property of one mine (in 1982), I actually experienced a car chase in which I tried to evade a company "safety" man sent to bring me back. I lost the "race." I was informed by the superintendent that I had trespassed and was asked to surrender the film I had shot. I handed over a blank roll instead. Several mining companies did allow me to photograph, not only on their property, but inside their mines as well. And at Wolf Creek Colliery, I was told by the man in charge, "My men on the old section are angry at me because you didn't take their pictures the other day. Could you please photograph them today?" He noted that production for the day had increased among the miners I had photographed. This was a strange role reversal. Usually it was the miners who were so receptive. At the first mine site I photographed, an old miner said: "A miner's life is a dog's life! Buddy, put that in your book!" And a young miner at Sycamore Mine told me: "What gets me is the pictures they show in the magazines of the men standing next to the machines—they are always smiling! Why don't you go inside and show it the way it really is!"

This book is dedicated to the Appalachian coal miners whose collective struggles for a better and more humane life have become an inspiring tradition, and to courageous coal miners all over the world.

Builder Levy

Images of Appalachian Coalfields

Introduction

The Appalachian region has served as the source for some of the
highest quality coal in the world, but the development of that industry never benefited the region's inhabitants as much as it did out-
siders—the speculators and the corporations who gained control of
the land and its minerals. From its earliest days, the industry has
been characterized by insecurity and exploitation. Intense competition for markets and frequent swings on boom and bust cycles created an economically vulnerable labor force and a deeply scarred
landscape. The history of Appalachian mining is a tale of continual
dislocation, a depressed regional economy, and volatile labor relations. Only in the 1960s have the political struggles of mine workers
resulted in some regulation of the industry and some protection for
workers.

This book is about the Appalachian coalfields during an important
time of transition—the 1970s and the 1980s. This introduction attempts an overview of the changes occurring in the workplace and in
the community and discusses the probable effects of coal industry
globalization on the Appalachian coalfields. The photographs, span-
ning fourteen years, show a beautiful region increasingly scarred by an

industry that has never demonstrated respect for the land or its people. And the photographs portray a community—a group of people who share a place and a history. Underground and in the camps, miners are bound by a sense of mutual obligation; traditionally, they have pulled together in times of crisis and they have endured.

WORKING IN THE MINES

Underground mining is hard and dangerous work, and until fairly recently no technology could substitute for human labor in extracting coal from the earth. Small-scale accidents and full-scale disasters—and respiratory diseases—constantly threatened miners' lives. The coal industry has been notorious for its lack of concern about worker health and safety. Improvements in working conditions came only after generations of miners fought for greater job security, improved safety in the mines, and health benefits, as well as for recognition of black lung disease as an occupational health hazard.

Beginning in the 1950s, new technology eliminated a great many jobs. Although the remaining jobs were safer and more secure and working conditions improved somewhat, the demand for coal was diminishing. As a result, the industry and some Appalachian communities contracted significantly until the energy crisis and the oil embargo of the 1970s brought new life to the coal industry. New jobs opened up, women in significant numbers entered the mines to work, and plans for industry expansion promised to lift Appalachia out of its long-depressed condition.

The Workplace

An underground coal mine consists of a few thoroughfares that branch into interconnecting passageways or tunnels that provide access to the working places. The main passages carry not only workers but electric power, water, ventilation, communication, and transportation facilities for coal and supplies. Small work groups of two to fifteen members enter the mine together, at the same time each day, and come out together. For the trip in, they travel in small buggies for as much as an hour before arriving at the small underground rooms where they will work until the end of their shift. In some mines, the workplaces are several miles from the entry. These damp and dark spaces in which the miners work vary in height from 24 inches to 21 feet. Most are less than 6 feet high. In mines of the past as well as in some that are still working, the work group is isolated from any outside contact, except for infrequent visits by a mining inspector, the operator, or an equipment salesperson or engineer. In more modern settings, there is more traffic, but miners do not leave their workplace until their shift is completed; they do not telephone outside and they take their breaks underground.

Although technology is rapidly changing the industry and working conditions, underground work is inherently dangerous; the lack of light and excessive noise from the mining machines limit communication among workers and increase the potential for accidents. In the large mines haulage routes are illuminated. In others only the battery-operated spotlights on the miners' hats or lights on the mining machines illuminate the workplace. Some mining machines require the workers to coordinate their tasks, but the noise created by the machines makes verbal communication difficult. Over the years miners have developed ways of communicating by means of lights so that they could work together and also warn others of impending danger. Isolated and interdependent, miners' work groups became efficient and close-knit teams, called section crews. Working with heavy machinery, on continuous miner sections or longwall, increases the necessity of coordination and cooperation among the members of the crew for maximum productivity and for safety's sake. Longwall mining, however, separates the workers and tends to lessen the traditional work-group solidarity. Miners themselves complain about the isolation and the lack of communication, camaraderie, and support on the longwalls.

As the news from mining regions around the world attests, mining accidents continue despite the modernization of work methods. In addition to the high risk of accidents, coal mines present health hazards associated with dust, fumes, noise, and other contaminants. The dangers are intensified by the close quarters and artificial ventilation. Miners are thus more likely than other occupational groups to die from respiratory diseases, stomach and lung cancer, and hypertension; they are also at higher risk of developing pneumoconiosis and bronchitis as a result of their exposure to coal-mine dusts. The monetary costs associated with miners' occupational illness are huge. From 1970 through 1983, the federal treasury paid $11.7 billion in such benefits, and the coal industry paid nothing, according to Curtis Seltzer in *Fire in the Hole: Miners and Managers in the American Coal Industry,* 1985.

The social costs are much greater, however. The number of workers who have died or who have been permanently disabled is so large that the economic base of many coal communities is derived from disease and disability compensation, but the consequences for the family and society are not easily quantifiable or even well understood.

Technology

In this century, sweeping technological changes in the production of coal have resulted in profound changes in the nature of the work as well as in the number of workers. Mechanization has also meant high capital investment, and hence the industry has tended toward concentration; that is, toward fewer producers controlling most of the production.

Originally, all coal was hewed and moved by hand. Using picks and bars, miners carved the coal from its solid bed, shoveled it into baskets, boxes, or wheelbarrows, and dragged it to the outside or to the foot of a shaft. By 1840, in Scotland and Wales, wheeled tubs on rails were being pushed by miners and pulled by ponies in the most modern pits. Cars were then developed to carry the coal. The earliest ones were drawn by humans, even children; later, by mid-nineteenth century in the United States, cars that rode on rails were pulled by mules, ponies, or horses. Then the introduction of black powder to blast down the coal further reduced the manual labor required (as it increased the dangers), but the skilled preparatory work of undercutting, sidecutting, and drilling could still be done only by hand.

The coal industry has always been highly competitive, and operators have sought technological change to cut labor costs and increase production. By 1900 some operations at the coal face were mechanized; punching machines and chain-type cutters were used for undermining the coal seam before blasting. But mining remained a labor-intensive industry until mechanical loaders were successfully introduced in the 1920s. Since then, mechanization and the development of new mining technology have rapidly advanced. Rubber-tired shuttle cars were introduced in the 1930s, and this innovation began the conversion from track-mounted loaders, cutters, and other equipment to off-track types utilizing crawlers or rubber tires, a much more flexible form. The mechanical loader raised miners' productivity by 20 percent between 1930 and 1950 and had an even more profound impact on coal production.

After World War II competition from alternative fuel sources like gas and oil reduced the demand for coal even for its traditional uses in transportation and heating. At the same time, the growing demand for low-quality coal from electric utilities created competition within the industry. The utilities could use the lower-quality coal that could be reached cheaply by surface mining operations. As a consequence, operators pushed harder to lower the production costs of underground mining by improving and extending mechanization.

In this period the coal industry was virtually revolutionized, and coal mining became more like an integrated factory system than a sequence of labor-intensive operations. For example, the introduction of tungsten carbide bits made it feasible to drill holes in rock to support the mine roof by bolting instead of with posts and crossbars thus affording more clearance for machinery, better cleanup, and higher productivity. The new bits were also incorporated into the cutting machines and continuous miners. The continuous miner was another important innovation of the 1950s: it rips coal from the seams, carries it by conveyor belt, and loads it on shuttle cars. It performs the cutting, drilling and blasting, and loading operations that had been performed separately by workers using conventional mining machinery. Between 1950 and 1960, productivity doubled from 6.2 to 12.1 tons per man-day. By changing the nature of the work the new technology altered the profile of the workforce. Most unskilled labor as well as many machine jobs were eliminated, while the demand for machine maintenance workers, mechanics and electricians, for example, dramatically increased. Conventional mining—drilling, blasting, and loading—produced 92 percent of underground coal in 1950; by 1978 conventional mining represented only 25 percent of underground coal and the continuous miner dominated the industry, producing 75 percent. As major companies adopted the continuous miner, or turned to surface mining, masses of coal miners were laid off indefinitely or for good. Between 1950 and 1960 employment of miners dropped by 60 percent, and the decline continued into the next decade. Between 1950 and 1970, the number of white workers fell from 483,818 to 128,275, a decline of

73.5 percent, and the number of Black workers, who were largely confined to the least-skilled jobs, plunged from 30,042 to 3,674, a reduction of 87.8 percent. Ronald L. Lewis's account of these changes, in *Black Coal Miners in America* (1987), is an excellent one. This period saw a steady exodus from the Appalachian coalfields as miners and their families migrated to northern and midwestern industrial centers in search of jobs.

As with production, underground transportation of coal has been increasingly mechanized. Various kinds of conveyances (e.g., a combination of shuttle cars and belt conveyors, or shuttle cars, belt conveyors, and track haulage) move coal through mines. Portable conveyors work behind the continuous miner or loading machine, and in recent years "scoops" have been used for loading and hauling in thin seams as well as for cleaning the floor and carrying supplies or men in all thicknesses of coal.

Modern mines are increasingly making use of longwall mining machines, which greatly improve productivity and efficiency. Longwall mining was used in some early mines until about 1910 but was supplanted by improved room-and-pillar methods, in which large blocks of coal are mined out, leaving "rooms" between the "pillars" or supports. When crews return to extract the pillars, they back out as they mine. This operation is called "pillaring." As other technologies were developed, however, interest in the longwall resumed. During World War II German engineers developed the longwall scraper for continuous loading of coal onto a chain conveyor at the coal face, and they later developed various types of shearing machines. An even more important innovation was the development of hydraulic, self-propelled roof jacks and chocks that greatly reduced the manpower required to set and reset individual jacks and build cribs by hand. Longwall mining now allows the recovery of about 90 percent of the coal in place, as compared with about 70 to 80 percent in room-and-pillar mining with pillaring and 45 to 60 percent without pillar recovery. Longwall mining also permits a high extraction ratio at great depths, whereas room-and-pillar mining becomes difficult and uneconomic at depths much below 1,000 feet because of high pressure on the pillars. Longwall mining increased productivity in terms of tons per man-shift. Although longwall requires a much higher initial equipment cost and increasingly requires purchasing rights to the surface to avoid lawsuits from dwellers whose houses crack or subside during or after the mining, some large-scale operations in the United States regard it as a key element in improving profitability. In a letter to stockholders accompanying the 1985–86 annual report, the president of Blue Diamond Coal Company explained the longwall method:

The longwall is a highly mechanized means of mining coal that has been greatly refined in the last five to ten years. It consists of a shearing machine, which hauls itself back and forth on a conveyor frame and cuts 30″ of coal from a 700′ face. Each longwall panel will be from 2,500′ to 8,100′ in length. The shearer and conveyor are both located under massive metal roof supports with hydraulic legs and most of the work is performed under these roof supports, greatly enhancing the safety of the work crew. On the longwall face, we are expecting to mine six times as much coal, with a similar sized crew, as on a continuous miner section. For this reason, the longwalls should make a significant reduction in the mining cost per ton at Scotia.

In the past few years, 108 longwall miners have been installed in the Appalachian area, and longwall production now represents 30 percent of the total production in West Virginia. Virginia mines average 79 tons yearly per miner on longwall as compared to 14.2 tons for all other mining methods, as reported in the *Energy Scout,* Virginia Center for Coal and Energy Research, for November 1986. Westmoreland Coal Company laid off 365 miners and Clinchfield laid off 250 after the longwalls were installed. As in the past, the new machines threaten marginally productive mines. Some of these have been eliminated and others have resorted to production speedups and lowered wages as they try to compete with the new longwall production. Workers in marginal operations face imminent job loss or increasingly hazardous conditions in the mines, as concerns for productivity overtake precautions for safety.

The New Miner
New technology requires new skill. No longer a pick-and-shovel operation, mining relies on a variety of work skills and the specialized training of many miners. These workers are entrants to the industry for operators have made no commitment to train their experienced workers in the use of new technology. Today's miners are younger and better educated than their counterparts of twenty years ago. In

1961 only 2.9 percent of all underground miners were under thirty years of age. In 1979, 41 percent were under thirty. Many of these young miners completed high school and some have been trained in mining at technical schools or community colleges. In 1980 the President's Commission on Coal estimated that three-fourths of entering miners have at least a high school education. In the 1970s, coal miners had begun to view themselves as skilled industrial workers or craftsmen rather than as laborers.

Today, union miners are paid annual wages ranging from $15,000 to $30,000, but their jobs are uncertain and still dangerous. The composition of the workforce is also changing. Since 1973 women have been entering it, and more than three thousand were hired as a result of pressure from women's advocacy groups and changes in federal laws regarding sex discrimination. In 1980 an estimated ten-thousand miners were Black, Hispanic, or Indian. In central Appalachia, however, the number of Blacks has declined. Blacks once represented a large proportion of the unskilled work force, but beginning in the 1930s and accelerating in the 1950s, when technology eliminated many of their jobs, Black migration greatly reduced the number of Blacks in the mines.

The Union

Coal miners were among the first industrial workers to organize, and they built a strong and militant union that has been a significant part of the larger labor movement in this country. The United Mine Workers of America (UMWA) led in the formation of the Congress of the Industrial Organizations (CIO). They fought for occupational health and safety and in the 1950s they developed a model health care system, establishing a series of hospitals throughout the coalfields. In the 1960s they used their power to get strong federal health and safety legislation with compensation for black lung disease. Today miners are struggling to maintain their past gains. A restructured, global coal industry is reshaping labor relations and contract agreements.

Labor relations between miners and operators have passed through many stages in the Appalachian region. In the twenties and thirties the battle for union recognition met great resistance from mine owners, resulting in mine wars in the Appalachian coalfields. (David Alan Corbin has written the history of these wars in *Life,*

Work, and Rebellion in the Coalfields, 1981.) But the miners persisted and developed a strong union.

It was at its strongest in the late 1930s and 1940s. The United Mine Workers, led by John L. Lewis, struck regularly during World War II, and the government used the national emergency provisions of the Taft–Hartley Act against the union three times between 1948 and 1950. Union members numbered more than four hundred thousand during Lewis's tenure. After the war economic changes pushed new technologies, which increased labor productivity. The union cooperated in the mechanization and new production techniques, with the result that American coal miners became the most productive in the world. But the increase in productivity also led to a decrease in the number of miners and a smaller and weaker union. (Curtis Seltzer's *Fire in the Hole* is an excellent account of labor relations in the American coal industry, and Curtis Harvey's *Coal in Appalachia,* issued in 1986, of the economics of the industry.)

The relationships between union leaders and miners changed in the 1950s. There were serious problems including autocratic rule, loss of democracy, and eventually corruption and murder. This finally led to union reform in the sixties through Miners for Democracy, which was formed to challenge UMWA President Tony Boyle. Much of the reform came from within the coal communities, and in December 1972 the reform candidate, Arnold Miller, formerly a leader in the black lung movement, was elected president of the UMWA.

The union then moved into a period of renewed militancy as union reforms and plans for growth in the coal industry following the OPEC oil embargo of late 1973 produced great optimism in the coal industry. The 1974 contract negotiations resulted in large wage and benefit increases, a cost-of-living escalator, important gains in safety, improvements in pension plans that included some disabled miners and widows. The industry agreed to the 1974 benefits, because operators and owners expected continued growth in coal consumption. This did not materialize, however, and they soon found many of the provisions intolerable. Declining productivity, due in part to the new safety regulations and a record number of strikes by miners seeking to enforce the safety laws led to efforts by coal management to reverse the gains won by the union in the 1974 contract. In the words of the operators, they were seeking to "stabilize" labor relations.

From the mid-1970s until the present the operators have sought to "reimpose stability and control" and increase productivity. The 1978 contract followed a 110-day contract strike, the longest national miners' strike in U.S. history, and the miners lost some of the hard-won gains of 1974, including the progressive health program, which was replaced by a company-by-company private insurance system. The contract gave management the right to fire, suspend, and fine miners for striking, picketing, or honoring picket lines, or in any way supporting wildcat strikes. In addition it eliminated many other restrictions in an effort to ensure productivity and profitability. The contract also represented a major drive to create an era of "cooperation" between labor and management, with joint committees to deal with problems of productivity and labor relations. The President's Commission on Coal was established to emphasize the mutual interest of miners and operators in "stabilizing" relations and increasing coal productivity.

The 1978 contract thus initiated a new era in labor relations that resulted in increased productivity and the virtual elimination of wildcat strikes. The operators' continued efforts to increase productivity and reduce high labor costs culminated in the 1981 contract, which opened the way for more non-union labor and coal. Miners began to see more concerted efforts by the operators to eliminate or neutralize the union. Many companies began selling out to non-union companies, or reorganizing the companies as non-union, or contracting with non-union producers, and more new operations entering the field were non-union.

In the mid-1980s the industry began another "shakedown" period, with marginal operations being sifted out. (Francis J. Rivers analyzed this process in a 1986 report to the Commission on Religion in Appalachia.) Steel company coal owners and land companies were selling their coal mines and reserves to large energy multinationals. When Rich Trumka became the UMWA president in 1982, he faced the problems of dealing with an industry being restructured and with the new multinationals. At first the industry cooperated with the new president to win approval of the 1984 contract without a strike, and the union developed a strategy of selective strikes against companies that refused to sign the contract agreement. This resulted in a major confrontation with one of the new multinationals, A. T. Massey, a Royal Dutch Shell-Fluor Corporation affiliate.

Massey is an example of the new multinationals and their style of operation. It has developed a form of decentralized management that seems to be the model for the industry. It has integrated sales but has separate relationships with different mines according to coal quality, thus combining small, decentralized producing operations with centralized worldwide sales and centralized capital, decision making, and planning. Massey refused to sign the 1984 contract, claiming that the small producing units were separate operations that could operate non-union. After a long strike the miners went back to work without gains, and the issues were not settled in the courts until 1988. During the strike, miners and their families found themselves facing armed security police with automatic weapons and trained guard dogs.

Like A. T. Massey, other new operations use a combination of new and old techniques to protect their interests. They use guards armed with billy clubs and machine guns and they use management consultants in three-piece suits with briefcases to wage psychological campaigns to convince workers that they "no longer need" the union. New mines are built and operated like armed camps, creating an atmosphere of fear and intimidation with modern security measures: chain-link and barbed-wire fences, floodlights, concrete block bunkers, and video surveillance cameras.

In the workplace miners face new style management and new controls over their work, such as new regulations for absenteeism and overtime. Miners say that it is not only the new technology that is increasing productivity, but also their fear of losing their jobs. Miners are making concessions to save their jobs and are working harder and longer—and many are working at much lower wages. All of this has had an adverse impact on safety. Since 1982 the fatality and permanent disability rates have increased. The highest rates occur in the small mines with fewer than fifty miners. These small mines, many of which are small contract producers for large multinationals, are the most vulnerable to market changes, have fewer training programs, and can least afford safety devices. Injuries also persist in the large mining companies, and some large multinationally owned operations have extremely high rates of death and injury. Today cost-cutting and the push for production result in less attention to safety and training, so that injury rates are high among many of the large companies as well. The *UMWA Journal* for March 1987 reported a 30 percent increase in coal miners killed on the job from 1985 to 1986.

A number of large companies are leaving the Bituminous Coal Operators Association, which has been the negotiating organization of the industry, in order to negotiate separately or become non-union operators. They are seeking changes in the contract that will give them the right to shift workers to different jobs, thus making workers more interchangeable. Management also wants more authority to hire and fire, eliminate affirmative action, institute longer work weeks, lower wages, and eliminate royalty payments for pensions—all ways to cut costs and make coal more competitive.

Island Creek Coal Company and the UMWA made a separate agreement, the "1987 Employment and Economic Security Pact." It is considered a gain by the UMWA in that it provides some job security: Island Creek will provide its employees first shot at available jobs in any new operation it opens or acquires, thus eliminating non-union contractors. The contractors must offer employment to laid-off Island Creek employees first. Island Creek had been notorious for using non-union contractors. The company calls the agreement a pact that balances "the employees desires for job security with Island Creek's goal of efficient operations and economic stability." The company no longer contributes to the fully funded and self-sustaining 1950 Pension Fund, which covers a small and ever-diminishing number of miners. While continuing to make full royalty payments to the 1974 Pension Fund, which covers most miners, Island Creek still saved $25 million in royalty payments, and the union gained greater job security and opportunities for its members without giving up any other gains.

The UMWA still includes a considerable percentage of mine workers, but because the large non-union strip mines in the West produce more coal with fewer workers, it controls only 40 percent of coal production. The union's powers are limited, in relation to multinational conglomerates with diverse holdings. These multinationals no longer depend on coal as their only source of profits and they can play one market against another. Many have both union and non-union companies and can shift production from one company to another. A growing number are following the Massey model and leasing to small non-union producing units. There has been a big growth in small operations since 1980, accounting for 36 percent of the Virginia operations and 24 percent of the Kentucky operations.

The UMWA is searching for new strategies to deal with these changes in the structure of the coal industry. The union is seeking new coalitions with other energy-related unions and has decided that it must work globally to fight global companies. Trumka and the UMWA led a campaign to boycott Shell and have advocated strong sanctions against South African coal and apartheid. The union is making linkages with the AFL-CIO, from which they split in the 1930s. UMWA leaders are very worried about the growing number of small non-union operations, and the decline in miners' standard of living, health, and safety. But with unemployment rates in many coalfield counties at about 50 percent, unemployed miners are taking jobs in these mines and working at the coal face for minimum wage. The union is also seeking alliances with community groups to fight against the concerted efforts of the coal industry to abolish all the gains the union has made over the past fifty years. For example, in November 1986, Mingo County, West Virginia, elections brought together a coalition of UMWA and coalfield community organizations to remove the A. T. Massey–controlled politicians and replace them with pro-union and pro-community officials, including some union leaders who had been fired by A. T. Massey. This effort is important not only to miners and their families but to all industrial workers.

COAL COMMUNITY LIFE
When coal mining began in the Appalachian region at the end of the nineteenth century, the companies had to find a cheap source of labor. Most indigenous farmers had little interest in the brutal work, so coal company agents went to Ellis Island and the Deep South to recruit workers. Housing was sparse in these rural areas, and existing towns could not absorb large numbers of new families. Therefore, the coal companies built camps to house their workers, and these company towns boosted their recruitment efforts. New immigrants and migrants as well as some hillside farmers, whose existence was meager and difficult, were attracted by the wages, company store goods, housing, and the excitement of the mining camps. When the ordinary means of attracting workers were insufficient for their needs, the companies also forced mountain farmers off the farms and into the mines by destroying farmland and water supplies and raising land values and taxes. Wages were good for those days—an average of one or two dollars a day—and many workers considered their situation a good one. But, for the former agricultural workers, an important change had occurred. They had been transformed from

independent small farmers to industrial wage workers and, like all miners, were now totally dependent on the company for which they worked.

The Coal Camp

Throughout the region, camps were built near mine sites. The mine entry, the tipple, or processing plant, the railway and coal cars, along with rows of coke ovens dominated the scene. The railroad was the only efficient means of transporting people and coal out of these isolated communities, and the houses were often built on both sides of the tracks. Managers and key personnel were favored with large and elaborate houses on spacious streets named "Quality Street" or "Big Berg Row," and the like. The workers were housed in another section in cheap look-alike buildings. Foreign-born and Black workers were segregated. They occupied separate living sections, and in many camps, schools and other facilities were also segregated. Most coal camps included an elementary school, a company store, and a church or two. Some added amenities such as a movie theatre, ball fields (for company-sponsored teams), a restaurant, and hospital or doctor's office.

Moreover, the border and internal space of the camps were closely controlled by means of company police, entry gates, and passes that limited entry and exit. Workers who were fired, lost their jobs, or were disabled could not stay; they were swiftly evicted and their credit at the company store terminated. When miners died in mine accidents, their families were evicted. The company store dominated the coal camp. Usually owned and operated by the mining company (or a corporation affiliated with it), the store linked the miner and family to the operator by strong bonds of debts and obligations. Although many miners attempted to continue farming on land leased from the company, the lack of land in some crowded camps often prevented them from having even the smallest gardens. Most families had to substitute the food and goods available at the store for the produce they were accustomed to growing themselves and their own household manufactures. Many families thus became totally dependent on the company store.

The store was usually housed in a large building associated with the company offices. In the early days of coal camps, wages issued as scrip served to tie the worker and his family to the company store. In the store, scrip held its value, but in town, miners' attempts to trade scrip brought only 90 or as little as 75 cents to the dollar. When legislation and labor contracts outlawed the use of scrip as wages, it was still used as an advance against wages earned but not yet payable or as part of a credit system.

The stores continued to be very profitable, and the use of credit expanded the company's control of the labor force, sometimes to an extent approaching peonage. But miners did not passively accept these conditions. Oldtimers in the camps still tell stories of community strikes against the management to improve living conditions, lower prices in the store, or provide community services in an attempt to open up and democratize the closed communities.

Visitors found little to like about the camps. The Boone report described camp life in the 1940s as "drab, bleak, leaving the population bewildered, idle, up rooted from the past, isolated from the mainstream of life flowing through a normal diversified community." Some camp residents had a similar view, remembering the camps as gossipy, dirty places with no privacy; their people were portrayed as wild and the conditions rough. Other residents, however, remember the camps as busy, booming towns in good times, with lots of friendly, helpful neighbors. One woman who grew up in the West Virginia coal camps recalls, "People were close and friendly. Women talked a lot over the fences and met each morning at the company store to draw scrip and buy groceries. The men talked a lot after work on the steps of the store."

In areas where towns predated the mines, mining companies and their workers soon dominated the local economy. The towns' fates became entwined with the miners. Layoffs, disasters, and strikes affected them all. Those who suffered or struggled together developed a strong sense of solidarity. In coal-mining communities, family ties were strong and a reliable source of support. Commonly family groups moved from farms to coalfields, and then used the family network to migrate to more prosperous areas. During depressions and periods when the mines mechanized, extensive networks enabled mining families to migrate to the cities and to return to the mountains during layoffs or at retirement. These networks have been an important source of support during mine closings, recessions, and strikes. Indeed, family members have always marched alongside the miners during coal mining strikes.

17

Communities in Flux

In 1947 a study of the health-care system in the coalfields was conducted by Navy medical and technical personnel directed by Admiral Joel T. Boone. The Boone report, *A Medical Survey of the Bituminous Coal Industry,* issued by the U.S. Government Printing Office, provided a portrait in words and pictures of the housing, sanitation, hygiene, medical care, and recreation of almost seventy-two thousand miners working in 260 mines—and their families. Its findings were that the coal counties had much higher infant mortality rates than the nation as a whole, that almost half the mining communities had contaminated water, and that medical care in the coalfields was inadequate—and, in many places, deplorable. Because of the Boone report, the UMWA built a series of hospitals in the Appalachian coalfields and developed a progressive industry-financed health program for miners and their families.

After World War II, and during the course of the Boone survey, however, other forces were dispersing coal miners and their families—and their communities. The coal companies began selling off camp houses to individual miners and camp stores to outside business people. The companies had found the camp houses expensive to maintain; selling the property to miners shifted the responsibility for taxes, repairs, installing and maintaining roads, water, supplies, sewage and garbage disposal facilities, and other public facilities and services. Moreover, mechanization in the mines after 1950 created a surplus of mining labor, and the companies no longer needed to provide housing and community services to recruit workers. Many houses and even whole communities were razed. As roads were built and miners acquired automobiles, there was less need for housing close to the mines. Workers could commute from nearby towns or buy land in neighboring rural areas. By the 1950s the population of the camps was reduced by half.

When the coal boom of the 1970s brought an increase in population and the demand for housing, the coal companies made little of their land available for housing. Mobile homes began to spring up throughout the area. Relatively well-paid miners lived in town or built comfortable houses outside the coal camps and commuted to work. Thus, the prosperity of the 1970s decreased the likelihood that miners working for a company would live in the same community and, thus, decreased the solidarity among miners and their families.

Some coal camps were demolished to make way for strip mining, while others became smaller home-owning communities made up of working and retired miners. Home ownership benefited some miners, but trapped others in the camps. With few opportunities for work in the mines and few alternatives to mining, the camps attracted no newcomers. Hence, residents could not sell their houses and move on. With so many miners out of work, some camps became "retirement villages." Others degenerated into rural slums. As a former resident, Clement Blanton, described the change in a 1972 study of the community (Clinch Valley College): "The once prosperous community is now a refuge for the poor; a dirty, cluttered depressed village with 200 and 300 persons. Only the school and church remain with abandoned mine offices and other buildings." Those who remained in the coal camps felt the loss of community spirit.

THE LEGACY

Since its inception in the Appalachian region, underground mining has adversely affected the land. Acres of slag remain on the surface while fires burn underground. Water sources have been polluted and streams have died from acid drainage. The new longwall methods of underground mining are responsible for problems of subsidence and damage to the water table. The greatest environmental damage to the region began in the 1950s when the increasing use of strip mining began to scar and level the mountains.

Strip Mining

Before 1941, surface mining of coal was limited to isolated pockets of very shallow coal seams, but after World War II, new earth-moving machines were converted from military use to coal mining. The larger and more energy-intensive strip-mining equipment made stripping profitable at greater depths and over a far wider area. Other factors also contributed to the growth of surface mining. The significantly lower initial capitalization and development lead-time for surface mines facilitated entry into the coal industry and encouraged new operations. Profitability was also greater because surface mining was more efficient than deep mining, removing as much as 80 to 90 percent of the coal in a seam rather than the 50 to 75 percent of conventional underground mining. Moreover, the use of non-union workers in most surface mines, along with relative freedom from safety requirements or restrictions on environmental damage, gave strip mining huge advantages over underground methods. At the same time, the technology for generating electricity was being modernized; the new generating units could utilize a cheaper type of coal than their predecessors. In the Appalachian area, the Tennessee Valley Authority (TVA) subsidized the development of surface mines to ensure a supply of cheap coal for generating electricity. It is ironic that the TVA, which was established as a development and conservation agency, helped to set the stage for a period of tremendously destructive strip mining.

The percentage of coal produced by surface methods increased steadily so that by 1975 approximately one-half of the 640 million tons of coal produced nationally was mined by surface removal methods. The development of surface mining also greatly increased the extent of operations in the West and created competition for Appalachian coal. Today the ten U.S. mines with the highest coal production are surface mines located in the West. By 1975 thousands of acres of farm and forest land were irreparably damaged, overturned, or buried. The soil and forest which covered the coal, called "overburden," were pushed into valleys and streams, resulting in floods, mud slides, and damage to roads, houses, and communities. Many miles of streams were polluted with silt and mine acid. Sometimes these mining practices took place despite the opposition of those who owned the land where mining was undertaken but not the mineral rights—they owned only the surface. "Broad form" deeds gave mineral owners the right to get the coal by any method they chose. These legal instruments had been supported by the Kentucky courts until a constitutional amendment was approved in November 1988 to prohibit their use. In other cases, privately owned land was destroyed by neighboring mining operations or operators intimidated owners into selling to them. Many were forced to move from the coves and hollows of Appalachia, and communities were devastated. Families were forced to move or live near spoil banks that ruined farmland, water, and roads, as homes and land were devalued. The operators, impervious to community and individual protest, claimed that they were benefiting the region by providing more flatland to encourage economic growth.

In areas where coal companies closed down their operations, remaining residents inherited a variety of hazards related to the abandoned mine workings. Underground mine fires, dangerous slag piles (such as those which caused the Buffalo Creek disaster in 1972), and burning coal refuse, or slag, endangered the whole community. Deserted mine structures, equipment, tunnels, and caves provided hazardous playgrounds for children. In areas where strip mining had replaced underground operations, they encroached on some small communities—water sources were destroyed and coal-hauling trucks spewed dust and damaged roads. The mines ruined the land, making it unfit for other uses. And when the coal was depleted, the companies abandoned these areas too, leaving the pillaged land to its residents.

Heightened political activity in the 1960s and 1970s led to the formation of such organizations as Save the Land and the People, Save Our Cumberland Mountains, and Virginia Citizens for Better Reclamation. These, along with older environmental groups and newly formed coalitions and national groups, began a serious political struggle that culminated in the 1977 federal strip-mine regulations.

A decade later, many of those who fought for the legislation claim that the law has never been properly enforced. Citizen groups must monitor the activities of the operators *and* the enforcers. Some coal operators believe the regulations are too stringent and hinder the industry, but even their grudging compliance with the legislation did make a major change in the way coal is mined and land is treated. For example, there has been an improvement in spoil handling and sediment control. During the seventies most spoil was shoved over hillsides and onto the downslope, creating soil erosion and flooding. Some say that the legislation "weeded out the renegades" and small, marginal operators, but others note that by allowing mountain-top removal, it resulted in larger operations, bigger machines, and a more drastic alteration of the landscape as whole mountain tops are now removed and flattened. And small operators (under 2 acres) were exempted from some restrictions, which opened the way to many abuses. Some companies even divided their operations into 2-acre ones in order to evade the regulations. Wildcat, illegal operations continue, especially in eastern Kentucky; these operations not only circumvent reclamation laws and safety regulations for their workers, but they pay no fees, taxes, or union royalties. Neither citizen groups nor federal officials have been able to curtail their activities.

Despite the limited compliance and irregular enforcement of the 1977 regulations, this legislation has had important practical and symbolic effects. The citizens organizations succeeded in getting both state and federal strip-mining legislation to protect their land and to help many families win compensation for damages. They demonstrated that collective action works and thus encouraged others to take a stand against a coal industry that most people believed was too strong to be affected by community protest.

The Coalfields Today

Recent changes in mining technology and the restructuring of the industry have created another wave of massive unemployment in Appalachian mining communities. In 1985, one-third of the UMWA's 105,000 members were laid off or were working short weeks. Thousands were searching for work. The UMWA says that 55,000 miners were unemployed in 1987. Between 1980 and 1986, 80,000 jobs were lost. From October 1985 to October 1986 alone, 15,000 jobs were lost, and the trend continues. The coalfields have the highest unemployment rate in the country.

Statistics from the state's Department of Mines and Minerals testify to the sharp decreases in the number of working coal miners in West Virginia:

Year	Employed
1950	117,500
1960	62,500
1984	41,300
1985	28,651

For the nation, mining employment dropped from 415,600 in 1950 to 177,800 in 1985, according to the Coal Data Book issued by the U.S. Department of Energy. The tremendous drop in the 1950s resulted from the introduction of the continuous miner; one-half the miners lost their jobs and left the Appalachian region. Losses in the mid-1980s, however, have occurred in a context of the decline in other industries such as steel and automobiles, and hence no major industrial centers are beckoning the unemployed miners. Some former miners have found employment in North Carolina, Georgia, and Florida, but many of their jobs are temporary. Those who do find permanent jobs discover that with living expenses so high and wages so low they cannot afford to send money to families left behind in the coalfields or relocate them to the new job locations.

This recent wave of unemployment in the coalfields has also produced greater inequities in coal communities, where residents include a small number of relatively well-paid miners, retired miners, miners' widows, and a growing number of unemployed and destitute miners and their families. In the Virginia coalfields, the official rate of unemployment ranges from 12 to 23 percent. Some 24 percent of the population in the Virginia coal counties alone lives on transfer payments—social security, disability, or black lung payments.

The human costs of these conditions are devastating. Many people cannot pay for health care, and the schools are full of hungry children again. The people caught in this spiraling poverty often do not see the changes as structural; instead, they feel inadequate and ashamed of their inability to support their families. The rates of suicide, alcoholism, drug use, domestic violence, school dropouts, and racist acts are all on the rise, while the literacy rate declines. These human costs are made clear in the testimony given at public hearings held by the Commission on Religion in Appalachia in 1985. The Commission published its findings in *Economic Transformation: The Appalachian Challenge* in 1986.

Having exhausted their unemployment compensation, many mining families are dependent on food stamps. Without jobs or land, mining families are even less able to care for each other as they have traditionally done during industry downturns or other crises. But they still try to pull together. Drawing on the creativity and resilience that enabled them to survive long strikes, layoffs, and depressions, many of the mining families are turning to an informal economy— bartering, selling goods, making crafts, and growing food. Women who have never worked outside the home are returning to school, seeking employment in the few small sewing factories, looking for low-wage jobs in nursing homes, or attending sick and disabled people at home.

In the midst of such hardship, miners and their communities are being asked to help make Appalachian coal more competitive by working for lower wages, cutting severance taxes, and giving up environmental regulations—in effect, subsidizing the industry. Having fought so long and hard for decent wages, safe working conditions, environmental controls and reclamation, equitable taxes, and some return to the community, miners and their families resist surrendering those protections.

There is, however, growing discussion of ways to provide more economic opportunities and choices for coalfield communities, to diversify the coal economy, and to encourage economic development that is more responsive to community needs. Community groups are considering reevaluation of their tax structures, especially when it comes to taxation of coal-bearing lands, and using severance taxes for economic investment in the region.

Mine worker and community experience has not borne out the companies' contention that what is good for the industry is good for miners and their communities. Between 1960 and 1980, the coal industry growth of 164 percent did not improve the quality of life in the coal communities. Industry prosperity did not raise incomes, jobs, tax revenues, or bank deposits. In fact, the growth cost the region. Road-repair costs for coal hauling alone were higher than tax revenues from coal producers, as indicated in the Mountain Association for Community Economic Development (MACED) report. With coal development, the economic "multiplier" works backward; there are few spin-offs. In fact, coal development discourages other development and burdens the community with costs. The MACED report of 1980, *Coal and Economic Development,* projected the costs of the coal industry to Kentucky over the next fifteen years at $1.5 billion. For years some workers and politicians in coal-mining states have persisted in the belief that coal industry growth and profits would ultimately ensure the development and economic well-being of the community. Today many of them are questioning that relationship. The current plight of mining communities is strong evidence that the enrichment of the coal producers has resulted in the impoverishment of the region and its people.

Helen Matthews Lewis

The Work

Some miners in this group whittle as they wait for the beginning of the afternoon shift. (Eastern Coal Company, a subsidiary of Pittston Corporation; Stone, Kentucky, 1970)

Brenda Ward. Women miners take an active role in their profession and have formed their own organization. As vocal critics of dangerous conditions and failures to enforce safety regulations, they have contributed significantly to improved safety for all miners. Also initiated by unionized women miners, and adopted by the United Mine Workers, is the contract demand for work leaves for new parents. (U.S. Steel No. 50 Mine; Pinnacle, West Virginia, 1982)

The morning shift waits for a "mantrip." (Wolf Creek Colliery, a subsidiary of A. T. Massey, now owned by Shell Corporation; Lovely, Kentucky, 1971)

Miners enter the mine on a "mantrip," the vehicle that transports miners into,
out of, and inside the mine, and, by extension, the term refers to the trip itself
as well. (Eastern Coal Company; Stone, Kentucky, 1970)

Pick-and-shovel work is still needed even in automated mines. (Wolf Creek Colliery; Lovely, Kentucky, 1971)

Two miners drill holes for the insertion of sticks of blasting powder (dynamite), which are used to loosen and break up coal at the work face. In today's mines, the use of "permissible explosives used in a permissible manner" that will not ignite the coal dust or the methane freed in the blast limits the dangers of blasting. (Bevin and Fauch Mine; Martin County, Kentucky, 1971)

A miner "shoots the coal," or detonates the blasting powder. (Wolf Creek Colliery; Lovely, Kentucky, 1971)

A section crew generally sets up a nearby area as a "dinner hole." (Harris No.
1 Mine, Eastern Associated Coal Corporation; Boone County, West Virginia,
1982)

Donna Ledsome (here with Jackie Davis) works as a supply Jeep operator. "I like my work, like the pay, and need the job." (Federal No. 2 Mine, Eastern Associated Coal Corporation; Grant Town, West Virginia, 1982)

Miners used to work alone or with a buddy, but today's miner is part of an interdependent, highly coordinated work group called a section crew. This crew is joined by an assistant mine foreman (*right*). (Wolf Creek Colliery; Lovely, Kentucky, 1971)

Roof stability—crucial to the safety of miners and machines—is achieved through roof bolting. Holes are drilled through the slate (shale) and into the more stable sandstone. Then long metal or resin expansion bolts are inserted in the holes and tightened, causing the bolt to expand and thus uniting several strata of roof materials into one large beam. (Federal No. 2 Mine, Eastern Associated Coal Corporation; Grant Town, West Virginia, 1982)

Before miners and machines work on a section, the roof bolters go in to set up temporary jacks and bolt the roof. In the old method of roof support, regularly spaced timber posts wedged between the floor and roof obstructed work space. The new method provides the open areas needed to operate the continuous miner, but even this improved support technology has not eliminated roof falls, still the leading cause of mine accidents. (Federal No. 2 Mine, Eastern Associated Coal Corporation)

The first revolutionary change in mining technology, the continuous miner,
combines in one machine the formerly separate functions of cutting, drilling,
blasting, and loading. Carbide cutting bits, mounted in rings or rotating cutting discs, literally rip coal out of the seam. The coal falls onto the gathering
head of the continuous miner, where the giant gathering arms sweep the
broken coal onto a conveyer that passes through the center of the machine
and discharges into a shuttle, or buggy. (Lightfoot No. 1 Mine, Eastern Associated Coal Corporation; Boone County, West Virginia, 1982)

Production was temporarily halted on this work section in order to free a rock caught in the loading conveyor chain of the continuous miner. Modern coal mining is high-intensity work done in periodic spurts with technologically sophisticated heavy machinery. The workplace is poorly lit and usually cramped; the roof is sometimes only 24 to 30 inches above the floor, though in some mines it is 10 to 15 feet high. (Lightfoot No. 1 Mine, Eastern Associated Coal Corporation)

Today's miner is more safety conscious, better educated, and better paid than his or her father or grandfather. (Wolf Creek Colliery; Lovely, Kentucky, 1971)

Rockdusting counteracts coal-dust explosions. Pulverized limestone is used to control the large quantities of fine, volatile coal dust that is created by the continuous miner and longwall machines. (Federal No. 2 Mine, Eastern Associated Coal Corporation; Grant Town, West Virginia, 1982)

Loaded coal cars in the mines, drawn by animals or men years ago, are now moved or "hauled" by motorized vehicles called "motors." (One of Eastern Associated Coal Corporation's mines; Boone County, West Virginia, 1982)

Several years after he was photographed, Andrew Kosto was killed by a large
piece of slate that fell as he was trying to locate an obstruction under the
loading tipple. (Sycamore Mining Company; Cinderella, West Virginia, 1971)

Working on the longwall in low coal, these prop mechanics must crawl through the dimly lit narrow space between the conveyor belt and hydraulic jacks. (Keystone No. 5 Mine, Eastern Associated Coal Corporation; Affinity, West Virginia, 1982)

The longwall machine on which this miner is working is like a narrow tunnel. The machine extends for the full length of the coal seam, which may be 1,000 feet long, but averages about 550 feet. A plow (for low coal) or a shear moving across the face of the seam cuts the coal, which then falls onto a conveyor belt. As the face is mined, the longwall moves forward, allowing the roof to cave in behind it. Thick steel plates (called props or shields) supported by hydraulic jacks protect the miners. (Keystone No. 5 Mine, Eastern Associated Coal Corporation)

Miners work under the shields of the longwall in high coal. (Federal No. 1 Mine, Eastern Associated Coal Corporation; Grant Town, West Virginia, 1982)

A prop mechanic will move jacks and shields forward as the coal face is mined
on this longwall in high coal. (Federal No. 1 Mine, Eastern Associated Coal
Corporation)

Dave Moore works at the head of the longwall. (Keystone No. 5 Mine, Eastern Associated Coal Corporation; Affinity, West Virginia, 1982)

A shear operator cuts coal on the longwall in high coal. Even with water
spraying, a cloud of very fine coal-dust particles forms, putting the miners who
breathe this at risk of black lung disease. (Federal No. 1 Mine, Eastern Associated Coal Corporation; Grant Town, West Virginia, 1982)

Workers emerge from the mine at shift's end. (Wolf Creek Colliery; Lovely, Kentucky, 1971)

Since the late nineteenth century, Black miners have been among the leaders in the struggle to defend and expand the rights of all coal miners. (Old House Branch Mine, Eastern Coal Company; Pike County, Kentucky, 1970)

Judy Poff returns her lamp and battery pack (for recharging) to the lamp house after working the "hoot owl" shift. A numbered brass tag identifies the place where her lamp belongs. A brass tag with the same number remains on her battery pack belt, which a miner always wears in the mine. Today many miners work overtime or double shifts, so that missing lamps at the end of a shift don't usually indicate a problem. After an explosion or other mine accident, however, a check of the lamp house will tell immediately who is missing inside the mine. (U.S. Steel No. 50 Mine; Pinnacle, West Virginia, 1982)

In this preparation plant, raw coal transported from the mine by coal cars or conveyor belts is separated from slate and other impurities. Then it is crushed, graded by size, washed, and dried. The coal is either stored or brought to the loading area, or tipple, where it is loaded on railroad cars, trucks, or barges for shipping. The entire preparation plant is sometimes called a tipple. (Keystone No. 5 Mine, Eastern Associated Coal Corporation; Affinity, West Virginia, 1982)

The coal waste—fine particulate matter including the fines or powdered coal suspended in water—is piped from the preparation plant into a refuse fines thickener, where the slurry thickens until it is about half water. A pump or conveyor transports the slurry to a dumping site—a sludge pond, worked-out strip mine, an artificial marsh, or a dammed-up hollow. The wastewater is recycled into the preparation plant. (Kopperston Preparation Plant, Eastern Associated Coal Corporation; Kopperston, West Virginia, 1982)

Miners with coal cars outside the preparation plant (Sycamore Mining Company; Cinderella, West Virginia, 1971)

Loading coal also disperses coal dust. This miner is not wearing his dust respirator. Some miners claim they have difficulty breathing through a respirator mask and do not wear one. (Eastern Coal Company; Stone, Kentucky, 1970)

A loading tipple stands behind the miners. (Smith Brothers Mining Company;
Williamson, West Virginia, 1971)

Before leaving the mine site, a truck loaded with coal stops on the truck scale at Westmorland Coal Corporation's Eccles No. 5 Mine. (Eccles, Raleigh County, West Virginia, 1982)

Generally, tugboats like this one on the Kanawha River pull loaded barges to transport coal. But this photograph was taken at the end of the 110-day national contract strike (1977–1978). Because of the strike, no coal was being loaded at the tipple, and no coal was being moved. (Harwood, West Virginia, 1978)

Coal en route (near Williamson, West Virginia, 1971)

Miners head home past the processing plant conveyor. (Kayford Branch Mine, Bethlehem Mining Company; Cabin Creek, West Virginia, 1978)

The Community

A coal camp near Grundy, Virginia, is a smaller settlement now than it was when the coal company owned it. (1970)

Since this photograph was taken in Osage, some of the houses have made way
for the construction of Interstate Highway No. 79. (Scotts Run, West Virginia,
1970)

Glenda Lee. In 1982, in Welch, West Virginia, another teenaged girl, Annia Castle, proudly told me: "I'm going to be a coal miner, too." (Pikeville, Kentucky, 1970)

Generations of miners have lived in company coal camps. Now this remnant
of a large camp is occupied by residents who do not necessarily work in the
mines. (Osage, Scott's Run, West Virginia, 1970)

Lee Holt's doorstep (Chattaroy, Mingo County, West Virginia, 1971)

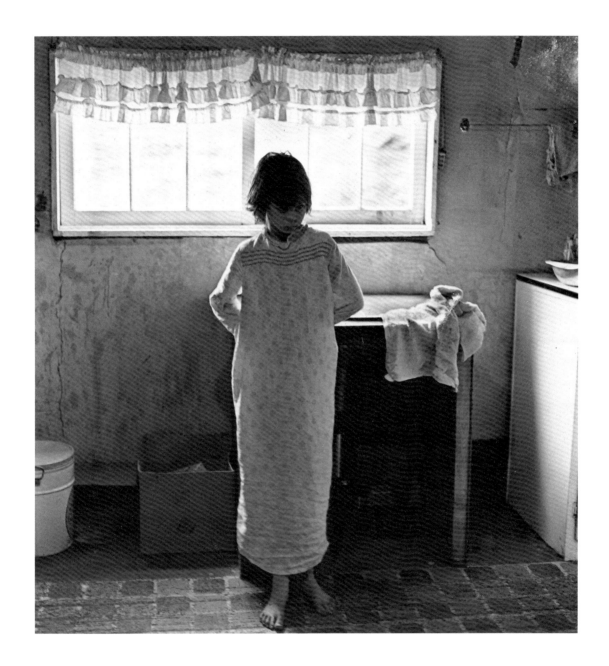

Donna Muncy (Crum, West Virginia, 1970)

The Johnsons with neighbors' children. George Johnson, a retired disabled miner, and his wife Grace rented my wife and me a room when we visited the area. (Chattaroy, Mingo County, West Virginia, 1972)

George Johnson took us along on a front-porch visit to Johnson's older sister.
(Myrtle, West Virginia, 1972)

The Riddle house is one of four remaining company houses in McAlpin, West Virginia. As residents moved out, the company tore down the houses. The coal company sold the remaining houses to a leasing company, which did no maintenance. Once Carl Riddle had seen my portfolio of mining photographs, he invited me into the house, to "photograph anything you like." Riddle and his wife Lorraine maintained the house for as long as they lived in it; Mr. Riddle moved from McAlpin into town after his wife died. (McAlpin, West Virginia, 1982)

The Oglesbys had also welcomed me into their home and offered me their hospitality. Luther Oglesby was a roof bolter who had worked in the mines for more than forty-four years. On Monday of the first week in April 1982, a notice had been posted at his mine: "No More Work Till Further Notice." He "worked that day and didn't work no more." He turned sixty that May. Dora Antoinette, the Oglesbys' daughter, stands in the doorway of her mother's bedroom. (Stotesbury, West Virginia, 1982)

The Oglesby kitchen (Stotesbury, West Virginia, 1982)

In the Riddle living room (McAlpin, West Virginia, 1982)

The table is set for Sunday dinner in the home of William Marcum, a disabled miner. (Between Williamson and Naugatuk, West Virginia, 1970)

Mae Phillips, a miner's widow, and her granddaughter Jeanne lived next door
to the family with whom I was staying. (Kildav, Harlan County, Kentucky,
1974)

This general store and post office probably once served as the company store for the nearby mine. (Clifftop, West Virginia, 1973)

Retired miners exchange cash for stringbeans. (Coxton, Harlan County Kentucky, 1974)

Charles Blevins' collection of musical instruments, mining tools, Indian gourds, and army weapons hangs on the wall of his Red Robin Inn, a small roadstop. (Borderland, West Virginia, 1971)

Retired miner Nimrod Workman, noted activist and writer and performer of
mining songs, gave his support to this project, introducing me to miners and
finding me a place to stay. (Chattaroy, Mingo County, West Virginia, 1972)

When Brice Mills, Jr. (*second from right*) was a boy, I stayed with his family. Mills is now a miner, too. (Everts, Harlan County, Kentucky, 1974)

At dusk in this small Mingo County coal and railroad town, some newsboys
congregate with their friends. (Kermit, West Virginia, 1968)

　　　　Vivian and Ellis Church and the family (Thacker Mine; West Virginia, 1970)

An imposing schoolhouse overlooks this old coal camp community. Because
of the richer coal seams in Pennsylvania, the greater strength of the union
there, and the proximity of Pittsburgh, the company houses (and schools) in
western Pennsylvania were sometimes built of brick instead of wood and were
generally more substantial than those in the southern coalfields. (Marianna,
Pennsylvania, 1973)

Montgomery, West Virginia, is one of many towns that prospered as a result of coal development. It is significant as the place where the Black Lung Association was born in 1968. Montgomery also is the home of the West Virginia Institute of Technology. (1978)

A coal truck navigates through the traffic on the main street of downtown Harlan, a major coal mining town in eastern Kentucky. (Harlan County, Kentucky, 1974)

Across from the railroad station are some of the buildings erected in the first quarter of the twentieth century, when this coal town was established. (Northfork, West Virginia, 1970)

In 1980, most coal miners (74 percent) owned their own homes, but 24 percent lived in mobile homes, compared to 5 percent of the general population. (Kanawha County, West Virginia, 1978)

Steve Kurilla has lived in this coal camp community for fifty-two years. He moved here in 1936 when he got married. In the 1940s the Kurillas bought the house from Ellsworth Collieries and since then the family has improved and remodeled it. (Ellsworth, Pennsylvania, 1973)

Michael Bonds gives his son Michael, Jr., a ride. (Stotesbury, West Virginia, 1982)

Camella Smith outside Della's Restaurant and Tavern (Rhodell, West Virginia, 1982)

Camella Smith at work inside

Most of the patrons of Montego Lounge—and all the people involved in this game—are miners. (Allen Junction, West Virginia, 1982)

Proprietor Douglas Stanley, who describes himself as "an ex-Kentucky moon-shiner and a disabled West Virginia miner," is aware of the lounge's impor-tance in the community: "Montego Lounge is the only place a coal miner or working person can go. We have the cheapest prices on liquor and no cover."

Participants in this Black Lung Association rally included John Mendez (*center*), chair of the Logan County Black Lung Association in 1971, and Ken Hechler (*second from right*), West Virginia's Secretary of State. (Lowell Phillips Kiwanis Park, Gilbert, West Virginia, 1971)

Also present at the rally were Dr. Donald Rasmussen (*far left, front row*), a
pioneer in diagnosing coal workers' pneumoconiosis, and Robert Payne
(*second from left*), president of the Disabled Miners and Widows Association.

Croatian immigrants formed a strong community in Cokeburg, Pennsylvania, and were the backbone of the miners' organization there. This couple attended the Miners for Democracy victory celebration picnic. (1973)

Other families at the Miners for Democracy picnic

The crucial support of miners' families, the Brookside Women's Club, the Black Lung Association, and other community residents helped the UMWA win recognition. (Brookside, Harlan County, Kentucky, 1973)

Striking miners outside the Highsplint mine. (Harlan County, Kentucky, 1974)

Harlan County is well remembered for its coal operators' violent suppression of union organizing. In the first major attempt to unionize miners since the 1930s, the United Mine Workers of America struck the mines at Brookside and Highsplint. Photographed on the day after Thanksgiving, 1973, these pickets were part of a thirteen-month strike in which one miner was killed.

Parishioners gather outside a church after services. (Mingo County, West
Virginia, 1970)

In 1908, one of the more "enlightened" coal barons, Major Tams, built a coal camp and opened and operated a coal mining company. He sold his company and property in 1955; a year later the houses were being razed to make room for new mine construction. Today, Slab Fork Coal Corporation's No. 10 Mine site, with a large preparation plant and supply yard, sits on the land that used to be the Black section of the camp. The New Salem Baptist Church, built in 1928 and wholly owned by Black Tams Camp residents, still stands and is operated by its loyal congregation. Many of the residents have since been forced to leave, but most of them have moved to nearby communities. (Tams, West Virginia, 1982)

A congregation gathers to save souls in "The Bottom," Keystone's redlight district. (Keystone, McDowell County, West Virginia, 1971)

105

Sunday services for another congregation and its preachers (Mingo County, West Virginia, 1970)

Fishing at the New River Gorge, Babcock State Park (Clifftop, West Virginia, 1973)

Over the bridge (Stotesbury, West Virginia, 1982)

The Legacy

View from Highsplint bridge (Harlan County, Kentucky, 1974)

Williamson, "Home of the Billion Dollar Coalfields" (Mingo County, West
Virginia, 1972)

Baseball has been an important part of coal-town life in southern Appalachia since the 1920s. Whether in county, United Mine Workers, or Black leagues, the great majority of players were miners. Until the 1950s nearly every town had a team, and some of the larger towns like Williamson and Beckley had Class-D professional teams. (Union Carbide plant, Alloy, West Virginia, 1978)

Small working farms still exist in Appalachia. Here sheep graze on a mountainside. (Between Marianna and Cokeburg, Pennsylvania, 1973)

Cows out in a snowstorm (near Farmington, West Virginia, 1970)

Coal has been strip-mined from these West Virginia mountains. The tops of
the mountains are blasted or bulldozed to expose the underlying coal seams.
If the coal is very deep, the mountain sides are stripped to get at the seams or
outcroppings; augers drill holes so that the coal can be extracted. Once the
mountains have been denuded of trees, heavy rains carry soil and debris to
lower ground. Floods and mud slides bring the mountain tops into the valleys.
(Bolt Mountain, Boone County, West Virginia, 1982)

Slag, or gob, another name for preparation-plant waste, can stay inert for years, then spontaneously ignite. Sometimes it burns for years, emitting sulfur dioxide fumes that endanger nearby residents. Slag fires are usually allowed to burn themselves out—about three hundred such fires are burning currently in Appalachia. (Logan County, West Virginia, 1972)

Waste separated from coal in the preparation plant is piped into an area that becomes a settling or sludge pond. Most modern plants also have a refuse fines thickener, but in small plants like this one, the sludge will be dredged out and trucked to a dumping site or to a worked-out strip mine. Acidic coal waste often seeps into and contaminates lakes, creeks, and rivers. (Kanawha River, Valley Camp, West Virginia, 1978)

Mounds of slag create a cordon around this mining community. (Ellsworth, Pennsylvania, 1973)

The Mount Olive Baptist Church is adjacent to the Wheeling Steel Corporation's preparation plant. (Stirrat, West Virginia, 1970)

A family cemetery adjoins the preparation plant for Nos. 25 and 26 Mines.
(Island Creek Coal Company; Ragland, West Virginia, 1971)

Local children use this abandoned tipple and its slag heap for play or solitude.
(Hickory, Pennsylvania, 1973)

Acknowledgments

In addition to the coal companies already mentioned in the captions, I wish to thank the following organizations and publications for their cooperation and help: *Coal Age; Coal Mining;* Coal Employment Project; U.S. Energy Information Administration, Department of Energy; Mine Safety and Health Administration, Office of Information and Public Affairs; U.S. Bureau of Mines, Department of the Interior, Pittsburgh Research Center; Miners Art Group; Highlander Educational and Research Center; Labor Research Association; and the International Center of Photography.

Beyond the generous people mentioned or pictured in the book, I want to express my appreciation and gratitude for help on this project to: the people of Harlan County, Kentucky, who made me feel secure during the tense time of the Brookside Strike, especially Gussie Mills for her kind hospitality, and to the people of Chattaroy, West Virginia, who made my wife Alice and me feel welcome during the summers of 1971 and 1972, especially the Johnson family for their abundant hospitality.

Gael McCarthy's editing advice and insights initially helped me transform my photographs and notes into a book. Dr. Paul Nyden was a rich source of information on Appalachian coal miners and a great help in making contacts throughout the coalfields. Arthur P. Sanda, a friend of Dr. Nyden, arranged my visits to several mines in 1982. I thank Harry Shaw for his friendship and the sharing of his extensive knowledge of Appalachian history and culture. The kind help of Art Shields, Mike Ross, Betty Jean Hall, Joseph Williams, and Ruth Lester must also be acknowledged.

My special thanks and gratitude go to the United Mine Workers of America and their President Richard Trumka for his early and full endorsement of this book project, as well as to Marat Moore, Dr. Lorin E. Kerr, Dr. Maier Fox, Joseph Corcoran, John Duray, and the UMWA *Journal* for the wealth of information they provided.

I also wish to acknowledge:

Cornell Capa and Dr. Helen Matthews Lewis for their important contributions to the book.

The staff of Temple University Press, especially Janet M. Francendese for her belief in my work and her patient and creative editing; Douglas Harper for his appreciation of my photographs; Mary Capouya for her sensitivity to the aesthetic needs of this book; and Arlene Putterman for her elegant design.

Drs. Walter and Naomi Rosenblum for their friendship, which enriched my involvement in photography and which led to this project.

The late Paul and Hazel Strand for their friendship and example, which helped make this book a reality.

Dr. Samuel D. Shrut for his friendship and guidance.

And my wife Dr. Alice Deutsch for her friendship and love.

This project was supported in part by a National Endowment for the Arts Fellowship grant, and by the generosity of my loving parents, Harold and Vivian Levy.